Jesus
The last week

Jesus
The last week

15 assemblies for secondary schools

Mike Anderson
Illustrations by Paul Heesome

Kevin Mayhew

First published in 2001 by
KEVIN MAYHEW LTD
Buxhall, Stowmarket, Suffolk IP14 3BW
E-mail: info@kevinmayhewltd.com

The material in this book first appeared in
The Complete Assembly Resource Book.

9 8 7 6 5 4 3 2 1 0

ISBN 1 84003 829 2
Catalogue No 1500469

Illustrations by Paul Heesome
Cover design by Angela Selfe
Typeset by Elisabeth Bates

Printed in Great Britain

Contents

Dedicated to the memory of those we miss most.

Overview

This project is based on a series of 15 posters. The idea is to create a sort of Lenten Calendar by adding a poster to classroom walls each day over the last three weeks of the Lent term. With each poster is a 'thought for the day' which could be read by either teacher or pupils together with a daily prayer.

However, the materials can be used in a variety of ways:

- A number of the 'thoughts for the day' could be selected to form the basis of a Lenten service.
- The illustrations could be photocopied onto OHP transparencies to be used in an assembly hall or chapel.
- The illustrations are modelled around a trinity of images and tones – some icons having specific parts to play. Identifying what each of them symbolises may form the basis of a discussion.
- The illustrations could be a springboard for a more penetrating study of the use of number and image symbolism so traditional in religious art.
- Discussing the roles may be the starting point for an empathetic written piece, pupils taking on the role of one of the figures in a particular illustration.
- This in turn could lead on to a piece of drama.
- Classes could reflect on the images, suggesting an appropriate symbolic mood colour for the message, e.g. a colour to reflect celebration, conflict, joy or hope.
- Pupils could be invited to design their own trinity of images to form the basis of a greetings card.

Although devised for use in schools, this project can be adapted for use in churches and Sunday school.

Whichever way the materials are used, we hope that in some way participants will have the opportunity to explore the most dramatic week in history – and be drawn to an encounter with Jesus.

1 JESUS – THE HERO!

THOUGHT FOR THE DAY

Has your local football team ever won anything? Even if they haven't, you will have seen football teams going back to their home towns the day after winning the FA Cup. Thousands of people wear the team's strip. They wave flags and scarves. They chant the names of the players and sing songs of triumph!

The last week of Jesus' life also started in triumph. He was welcomed into Jerusalem by people who really thought he was someone special. They had heard how he had helped people and performed miracles, and they wanted him to use his power to set them free from the Romans, who had occupied Israel. They wanted Jesus to use his powers for them.

Maybe we, too, fall into the same trap of expecting Jesus to do things for us. Maybe we think that if we pray, everything will go all right for us in life, that we'll pass our exams, get good jobs and live happily ever after. Life is rarely that simple!

Perhaps we should think less about what Jesus can do for us – and more about what we can do for others. That's being a hero!

JESUS – THE HERO!

A FEW SECONDS OF SILENT REFLECTION

PRAYER

Good is stronger than evil.
Love is stronger than hate.
Light is stronger than darkness.
Life is stronger than death.
Victory is ours –
through him who loves us.
Amen.

Desmond Tutu

1 JESUS – THE HERO!

2 JESUS – THE SERVANT

THOUGHT FOR THE DAY

Jesus washes his friends' feet

Are you a selfish person? The answer will probably be, 'No – of course not!'

However, maybe there is one area of your life where you are a bit selfish. Maybe you expect your mum to tidy your room. Maybe you expect to get whatever you want for your birthday. Maybe you expect your tea to be cooked for you. Maybe you expect your clothes to be washed and ironed for you.

Today, we think about how Jesus showed us that it was important to care for others in the really practical things of life. He – the leader – washed the feet of his disciples, to show that we should not expect to be waited on hand and foot, but that we should do what we can to make life better for others.

Maybe that could be your challenge for today – to DO something for someone else that you don't normally do.

JESUS – THE SERVANT

A FEW SECONDS OF SILENT REFLECTION

PRAYER

Good is stronger than evil.
Love is stronger than hate.
Light is stronger than darkness.
Life is stronger than death.
Victory is ours –
through him who loves us.
Amen.

Desmond Tutu

2 JESUS – THE SERVANT

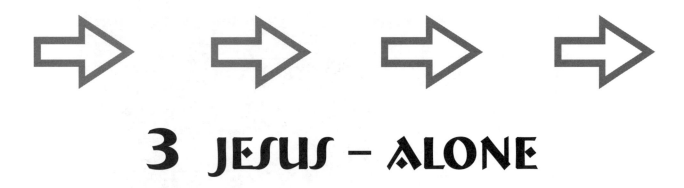

3 JESUS – ALONE

THOUGHT FOR THE DAY

Jesus prays in the Garden of Gethsemane, while his disciples sleep

Have you ever been 'stood up' – arranged to meet someone and they've not turned up? Have you ever been let down by someone who promised to do something for you, or who promised to support you in some way but didn't?

Imagine how Jesus felt when he asked his friends to pray for him. They had seen him perform miracles. They had seen him walk on water. And yet, they fell asleep. It is easy to feel sympathy for Peter, James and John. After all, it was late – and they had just had a good meal and drunk some wine. Nevertheless – they let Jesus down – even though they didn't mean to.

Maybe you could make a special effort not to let anyone down in any way today. Maybe you could make a special effort today to include someone in your group who seems a bit lonely.

JESUS – ALONE

A FEW SECONDS OF SILENT REFLECTION

PRAYER

Good is stronger than evil.
Love is stronger than hate.
Light is stronger than darkness.
Life is stronger than death.
Victory is ours –
through him who loves us.
Amen.

Desmond Tutu

3 JESUS – ALONE

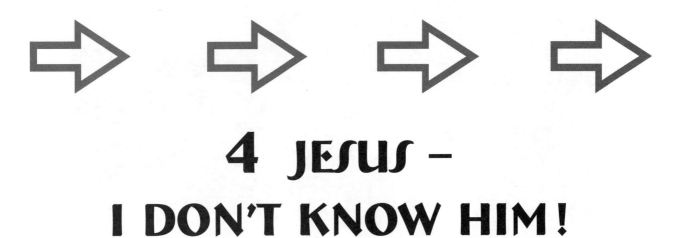

4 JESUS –
I DON'T KNOW HIM!

THOUGHT FOR THE DAY

Peter denies Jesus three times

This is one of the most famous stories in the Gospels. Peter pretends that he doesn't know Jesus. Basically, he lies – three times. The very fact that it was three times suggests that it was no mistake. When Peter said he didn't know Jesus the first time, it was to a servant girl. Then, when others asked him about it, he had to continue the lie until, finally, he had to shout that he didn't know Jesus.

Lying gets out of hand very easily. It can start with saying we have forgotten our homework, when really we haven't done it. It can move on to saying that your mum is writing you a note about it. It can continue with saying that your Year Head wants to see you, when you are supposed to be at break-time detention, and so on.

Maybe today we can all resolve to speak the truth, even if it means we get into trouble.

JESUS – I DON'T KNOW HIM!

A FEW SECONDS OF SILENT REFLECTION

PRAYER

Good is stronger than evil.
Love is stronger than hate.
Light is stronger than darkness.
Life is stronger than death.
Victory is ours –
through him who loves us.
Amen.

Desmond Tutu

4 JESUS –
I DON'T KNOW HIM!

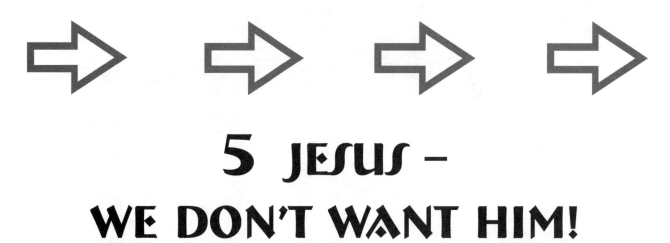

5 JESUS – WE DON'T WANT HIM!

THOUGHT FOR THE DAY

The crowd shout for Barabbas to be freed

Does your class or group of friends sometimes deliberately exclude someone and make life unhappy for them? Sometimes it starts because someone is given a nickname and everyone latches onto it and uses it abusively. It's often done in a sly, snide way, which undermines a person's confidence. The victim feels 'got at', left out and their self-esteem hits rock bottom.

Can you imagine how Jesus must have felt when the crowd chose to have Pilate free Barabbas – a murderer – instead of him? Surely some of these people were the same ones who had acclaimed him a hero when he came into Jerusalem. But they had been 'got at' by the chief priests and were too afraid to go against them.

Maybe your challenge could be to stand up for a victim next time you see someone being verbally or emotionally bullied.

JESUS – WE DON'T WANT HIM!

A FEW SECONDS OF SILENT REFLECTION

PRAYER

Good is stronger than evil.
Love is stronger than hate.
Light is stronger than darkness.
Life is stronger than death.
Victory is ours –
through him who loves us.
Amen.

Desmond Tutu

5 JESUS –
WE DON'T WANT HIM!

6 JESUS – NOTHING TO DO WITH ME

THOUGHT FOR THE DAY

Jesus before Pilate, who washes his hands

There is a series of adverts on the TV for Special Constables. One of them involves a group of youngsters roughing up a schoolboy in uniform. Most people just walk on by – they're too frightened to get involved.

In the same way, Pilate had the power to prevent Jesus being crucified, but he did literally 'wash his hands', as if that meant he wouldn't get the blame. However, the story of Pilate is still known and he is blamed 2,000 years later for allowing Jesus to die.

There are situations where we can step in and stop something wrong happening, and today we are challenged to do that. A simple way to do this is to think of the Third World. It's easy to say, 'It's nothing to do with me', but we shouldn't. Why not think about how you can help raise some money for CAFOD or some other charity this week, to show that you are not 'washing your hands' of the responsibility for those who suffer?

JESUS – NOTHING TO DO WITH ME

A FEW SECONDS OF SILENT REFLECTION

PRAYER

Good is stronger than evil.
Love is stronger than hate.
Light is stronger than darkness.
Life is stronger than death.
Victory is ours –
through him who loves us.
Amen.

Desmond Tutu

 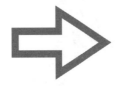 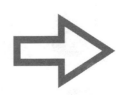 

6 JESUS –
NOTHING TO DO WITH ME

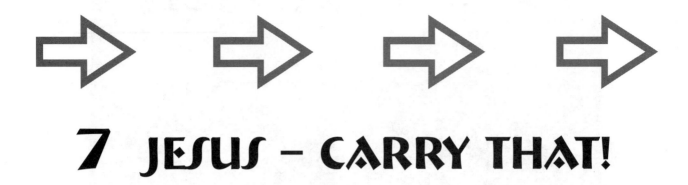

7 JESUS – CARRY THAT!

THOUGHT FOR THE DAY

Jesus receives the cross

We have all got something in our lives that weighs us down. It may be a health problem, a relationship problem, a death in the family, a dissatisfaction with our appearance or weight, worries over money, concerns over what our parents expect of us, and so on. These can all be difficult crosses to bear.

Jesus had to carry a large wooden cross-beam. The traditional image of Jesus carrying a full cross is probably incorrect, as it was customary at that time to have the vertical part of a cross fixed permanently into the ground. The cross-beam would then be hauled up the vertical part to form the cross shape.

Jesus had to accept something that wasn't fair. It wasn't fair that he should be given the cross. It's not fair that some people have more difficult crosses to bear than others. Maybe today's challenge could be to make sure we don't add to anyone's cross by what we say, or do or don't do.

JESUS – CARRY THAT!

A FEW SECONDS OF SILENT REFLECTION

PRAYER

Good is stronger than evil.
Love is stronger than hate.
Light is stronger than darkness.
Life is stronger than death.
Victory is ours –
through him who loves us.
Amen.

Desmond Tutu

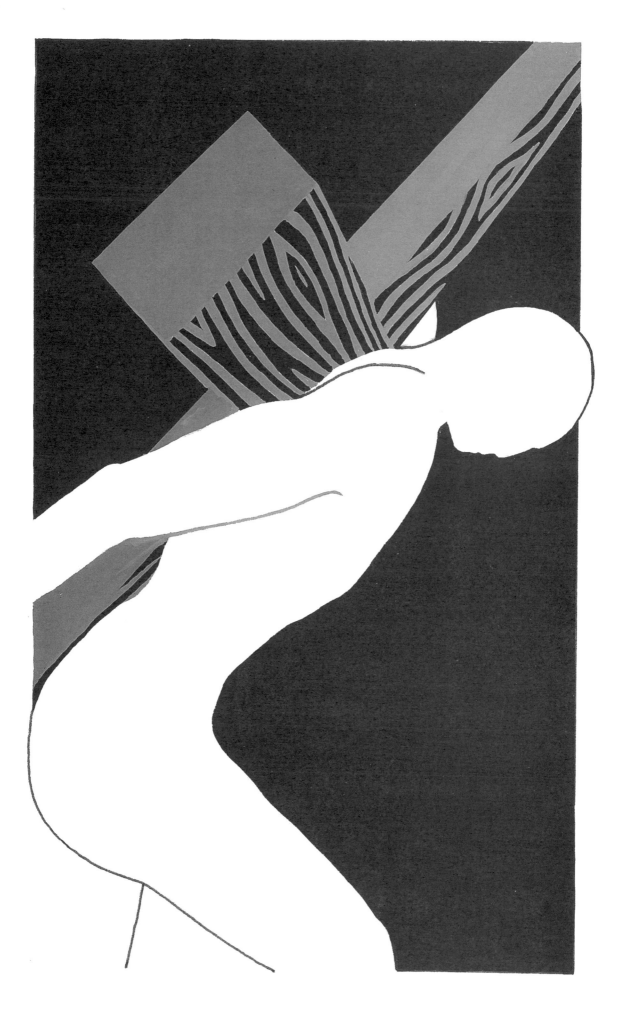

7 JESUS – CARRY THAT!

8 JESUS – THE WEAKLING

THOUGHT FOR THE DAY

Simon of Cyrene carries the cross of Jesus

Jesus became so weak that the soldiers were afraid he was going to die before he could be crucified. So they grabbed Simon of Cyrene out of the crowd and made him carry the cross-beam for Jesus. Maybe you didn't realise that this was probably a case of racial discrimination, because Simon of Cyrene was almost certainly black. The soldiers picked him – an African – out of the crowd and forced him to help Jesus.

Simon probably didn't see it as an honour to help Jesus. As a stranger in Jerusalem, he wouldn't have known what was going on. And yet his name has been remembered for 2,000 years. While he didn't see it as an honour to help Jesus at the time, it seems that this experience had a profound effect on Simon – so much so that his name was written in the Gospels, which were written more than 30 years later.

Sometimes, when we're asked to help others in some way, we resent it – maybe we throw a strop when asked to go to the shops or clean our room. Our challenge today is to help others willingly.

A FEW SECONDS OF SILENT REFLECTION

PRAYER

Good is stronger than evil.
Love is stronger than hate.
Light is stronger than darkness.
Life is stronger than death.
Victory is ours –
through him who loves us.
Amen.

Desmond Tutu

JESUS – THE WEAKLING

8 JESUS – THE WEAKLING

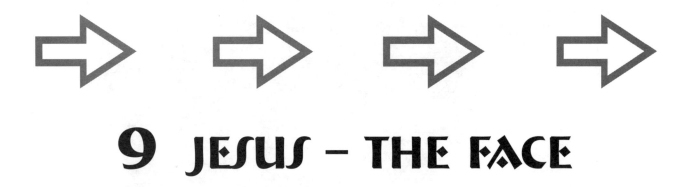

9 JESUS – THE FACE

THOUGHT FOR THE DAY

Veronica wipes the face of Jesus

Although there is no mention of it in the Gospels, there is a Church tradition that a woman called Veronica was so overcome to see Jesus suffering that she burst through the line of soldiers escorting him and wiped the face of Jesus on his journey to Golgotha. This tradition suggests that a full photographic imprint of the face of Jesus was left on the cloth used.

Have you ever wondered what Jesus must have looked like? European Christians tend to think of Jesus as being tall, slim, and white, with long straight hair, a beard and piercing eyes. African Christians picture Jesus as a black man. Chinese Christians think of Jesus as having oriental features.

Today, though, think to yourself – 'Has Jesus made any impression on my life?' If not, perhaps you need to think about how you can help Jesus, like Veronica was thought to have done. Of course, you can't help Jesus directly, but maybe you can help someone else. In helping them – you are helping Jesus.

JESUS – THE FACE

A FEW SECONDS OF SILENT REFLECTION

PRAYER

Good is stronger than evil.
Love is stronger than hate.
Light is stronger than darkness.
Life is stronger than death.
Victory is ours –
through him who loves us.
Amen.

Desmond Tutu

9 JESUS – THE FACE

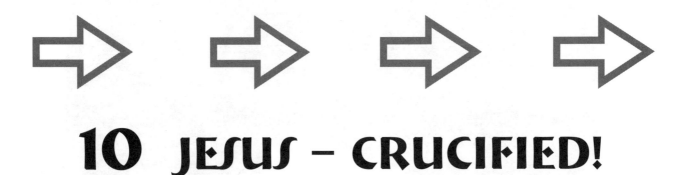

10 JESUS – CRUCIFIED!

THOUGHT FOR THE DAY

Having reached Golgotha ('the Place of the Skull'), Jesus was nailed to the cross. The crude nails used would have been about six inches long and would almost certainly have been hammered in through the wrist and not the palm of the hand. A nail driven through the palm would have ripped through the hand tissue and would not keep the victim on the cross.

As the nails were driven in, Jesus said: 'Father – forgive them – they don't know what they're doing.'

This gives some idea of how deeply Jesus loved everyone. There is a story about a Roman soldier who met Jesus. The soldier asked, 'You talk about loving enemies as well as friends. Well, I am a soldier who oppresses your people – who despises your Jewish religion. How much do you love me?'

And Jesus replied: 'This much!' And he stretched out his arms and they nailed him to the cross.

JESUS – CRUCIFIED!

A FEW SECONDS OF SILENT REFLECTION

PRAYER

Good is stronger than evil.
Love is stronger than hate.
Light is stronger than darkness.
Life is stronger than death.
Victory is ours –
through him who loves us.
Amen.

Desmond Tutu

10 JESUS – CRUCIFIED!

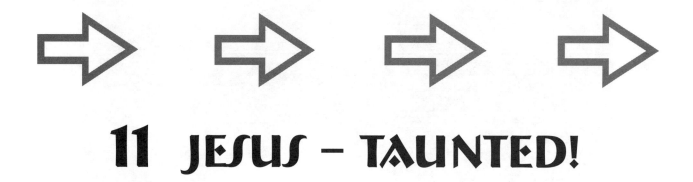

11 JESUS – TAUNTED!

THOUGHT FOR THE DAY

Have you ever had anyone rub it in when you've done something daft? Have you ever had someone really put the boot in when you're already feeling rotten? Maybe you've made someone else feel bad by what you've said, by verbally abusing them.

Charles Dickens once said: 'There is a great man who makes others feel small, but the really great man is the one who makes other people feel big.' Sometimes we use our mouths to belittle others – to make them feel small or soft or useless.

Even when Jesus was on the cross, three groups of people taunted him. They were the chief priests (religious people), the soldiers and the passers-by. He was dying, but they couldn't resist the temptation to have a laugh at Jesus.

Today's challenge is for us to resist the temptation to skit or belittle others.

JESUS – TAUNTED!

A FEW SECONDS OF SILENT REFLECTION

PRAYER

Good is stronger than evil.
Love is stronger than hate.
Light is stronger than darkness.
Life is stronger than death.
Victory is ours –
through him who loves us.
Amen.

Desmond Tutu

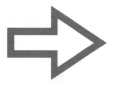
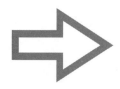

11 JESUS – TAUNTED!

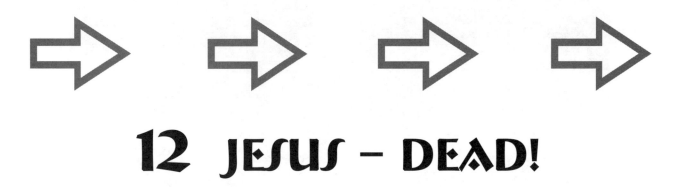

12 JESUS – DEAD!

THOUGHT FOR THE DAY

Finally, after six hours on the cross, Jesus cried out: 'Eloi, eloi, lama sabachtani?' which means 'My God, my God, why have you abandoned me?'

Many people think that this was Jesus in despair – thinking that God had given up on him. However, these words are the first words of Psalm 22, which was a song describing how Yahweh (the Jewish name for God) would save all who were suffering, and change the world into a better place. It is a song of triumph.

So, Jesus' final words are not a cry of despair. Jesus was singing a song of victory.

JESUS – DEAD!

A FEW SECONDS OF SILENT REFLECTION

PRAYER

Good is stronger than evil.
Love is stronger than hate.
Light is stronger than darkness.
Life is stronger than death.
Victory is ours –
through him who loves us.
Amen.

Desmond Tutu

12 JESUS – DEAD!

13 JESUS – BURIED

THOUGHT FOR THE DAY

Jesus is placed in the tomb

We all have had bad things happen to us, things we prefer not to think about. We try to put them at the back of our minds and forget about them. But every now and again the memories flood back and we relive the experience.

Imagine how the followers of Jesus felt as his body was taken from the cross and put in the tomb. They must have thought that their great adventure with Jesus was over. They must have thought it was all pretty pointless and perhaps wanted to put it out of their minds. It was not a time for rejoicing – or celebrating. It was a time for sadness. Maybe some of them (like Peter) were thinking about what they wanted to say to Jesus before he died. Maybe they felt guilty about running away. Maybe they were saying to themselves: 'If only I'd stood by him'; 'If only I'd stayed awake in the Garden, I could have warned him'; 'If only I'd carried his cross for him'; 'If only I'd . . .'

Why not take the chance today to do something you should have done, or say something you should have said – so that you won't have to say, 'If only I'd . . .'

A FEW SECONDS OF SILENT REFLECTION

PRAYER

Good is stronger than evil.
Love is stronger than hate.
Light is stronger than darkness.
Life is stronger than death.
Victory is ours –
through him who loves us.
Amen.

Desmond Tutu

JESUS – BURIED

13 JESUS – BURIED

14 JESUS – WHERE IS HE?

THOUGHT FOR THE DAY

The empty tomb

Have you ever watched *The X-Files*? It can be really scary in an exciting sort of way. Have you ever been somewhere really spooky – where you're almost too scared to stay but too frightened to move on? Have you ever had the experience of being in a little world of your own, when someone walks in and gives you a tremendous shock that makes your heart pound?

The women who went to Jesus' tomb, very early on the Sunday morning after he'd been buried, had just such an experience. It would have been a bit dark and cold, because it was very early. They (we're not sure whether there were two or three of them – the Gospels don't agree) were walking through a graveyard. No one else would have been around. As they approached the tomb, they saw the stone covering the entrance had been rolled away. What would you have done? Would you have walked in? Would you have said: 'After you, Mary'? Would you have been frightened?

Anyway, the women did go in (according to Luke), and Jesus' body had gone.

And then – out of nowhere – two men appeared. Can you imagine how the women would have jumped? The men told them that Jesus had risen from the dead. Would you have believed them?

JESUS – WHERE IS HE?

A FEW SECONDS OF SILENT REFLECTION

PRAYER

Good is stronger than evil.
Love is stronger than hate.
Light is stronger than darkness.
Life is stronger than death.
Victory is ours –
through him who loves us.
Amen.

Desmond Tutu

14 JESUS – WHERE IS HE?

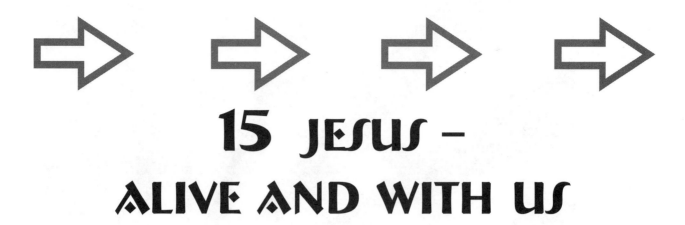

15 JESUS – ALIVE AND WITH US

THOUGHT FOR THE DAY

Jesus appears to the disciples but they do not recognise him

Have you ever met someone whose face you recognise, but you can't quite place them? As you get older it seems to happen more and more! After you've left school, you'll see your ex-teachers in town and maybe say 'Hello' to them – and be faced with a rather glazed look and furrowed brow as they try to dig up your name from their memory banks.

The Gospels tell slightly different stories about what happened after Jesus rose from the dead, but one fairly common feature of these stories is that his followers do not recognise him immediately. Was that because they were not expecting to see him? Was it because he had changed in some way? We don't really know.

What does happen, though, is that they recognise Jesus in his actions and words. We too should not expect to see Jesus face to face. Would we recognise him anyway? However, we can meet Jesus whenever someone does something that Jesus would have done. We meet Jesus in acts of kindness – in words of justice and peace – we meet Jesus in each other, when we do what Jesus would have done.

Try to see the risen Jesus in someone else today. And look in the mirror and see if you are sometimes Jesus to someone else – through what you say and do.

Enjoy your Easter Holidays!

JESUS – ALIVE AND WITH US

A FEW SECONDS OF SILENT REFLECTION

PRAYER

Good is stronger than evil.

Love is stronger than hate.

Light is stronger than darkness.

Life is stronger than death.

Victory is ours –

through him who loves us.

Amen.

Desmond Tutu

15 JESUS –
ALIVE AND WITH US

PRAYER

Good is stronger than evil.

Love is stronger than hate.

Light is stronger than darkness.

Life is stronger than death.

Victory is ours –

through him who loves us.

Amen.

Desmond Tutu